A Butterfly's Evening Adventure

This course was written by
Naturally Curious Expert
Kira Freed

*Kira used to be an archaeozoologist. Now she
writes science materials for children. She is curious
about all the different forms of life in our world.*

Printed by CreateSpace

ISBN 978-1-942403-00-5

www.benaturallycurious.com

Many activities in this book make use of printed materials. If you prefer not to cut them directly from this book, please visit the URL listed below and enter the code for a supplemental PDF containing all printable materials.

URL: www.benaturallycurious.com/butterfly-adventure-printables/

password: **wings**

Table of Contents

Required Materials

- Three opaque cups
- Paper and pencil for scoring
- Scissors
- Glue or tape (possibly double-sided tape)
- Lightweight cardboard (e.g., cereal box flap)
- Nylon fishing line
- Hole punch (or a paper clip)
- String
- Notepad

- Pocket or phone camera (optional)
- Crayons, colored pencils, or markers (optional)
- Beads, sequins, and yarn or colored string (optional)
- Wooden embroidery hoop (optional)
- One neutral-colored T-shirt for each player*
- One brightly colored T-shirt for each player*

*T-shirts should have the same length of sleeves (both short or both long).

Bella the Butterfly Meets Morty the Moth

This is a story about a butterfly named Bella. Meet Bella. She's a question mark butterfly. You're probably thinking that's a funny name for a butterfly, but that's really what she's called. (Don't laugh—one of her cousins is called a comma butterfly!)

Bella lives in a wooded area near a city park. She spends her time flying around, playing with her friends, and enjoying her favorite foods, which include tree sap, rotten fruit, and animal poop. (Really.)

Bella is different from her friends in one important way. (But she may be just like you in this way!) She is a very, very curious butterfly. She always wants to know more about the world around her. One day, she learned a LOT more than she expected to learn!

That afternoon, Bella asked her mom, "Can I go outside and play with my friends?"

Bella's mom replied, "Yes, of course—just make sure you're home before dark." She gave Bella a butterfly kiss and said, "Have fun!"

Bella flew off to play with her friends. They decided to play hide-and-seek in the woods. After they played for a while, it was Bella's turn to hide. She wanted to find a really good hiding place, so she flew higher than usual.

Suddenly, Bella spotted something interesting. "Hey—what's that?" she wondered. Bella saw an empty bird's nest! She thought to herself, "What a great place to hide from my friends. They'll never find me here!"

Although Bella's wings were bright orange on the outside, they were brown on the undersides—the exact same color as the nest! Bella held her wings up and together to hide the orange. Using color this way is a type of CAMOUFLAGE called BLENDING COLORATION. (She blended in with the color of the nest.) Bella stayed really still, waiting for her friends to come looking for her.

Bella waited … and waited … and waited, but nobody came! All of a sudden, she noticed that it was getting dark. Bella had never been away from home after dark before. She didn't think she could find her way home in the dark.

Bella was scared—*really* scared. She stayed in the nest, too scared to leave. Before long, she started crying. What if she had to stay there all night?

Suddenly, Bella heard a soft whirring noise. Something landed near her on the branch! What could it be? "Who's there?" she called out timidly.

A friendly face peered over the edge of the nest. It looked a little like Bella's face, but different. *Fuzzy* different! "Hey, who are you?" the fuzzy creature asked.

"I'm Bella. I'm a question mark butterfly. I stayed out too late, and now I don't know how to get home in the dark. I'm a DIURNAL insect—I'm only supposed to be active during the day."

Bella's visitor hopped up on the edge of the nest to see her better. "Wow!" he said. "I never met a diurnal insect before! I'm NOCTURNAL—I'm only active at night. It's very nice to meet you, Bella. I'm a moth—a white-lined sphinx moth. My name is Mortimer, but my friends call me Morty."

Blending coloration is a type of *camouflage*. It helps an animal blend in with the background.

A *diurnal* animal is active during the day. Most butterflies are diurnal.

A *nocturnal* animal is active at night. Most moths are nocturnal.

"Hi, Morty. I've heard of moths, but I never met one before! You look kind of like me but also really different. Your ANTENNAE are fuzzy, and so is your face!"

Morty looked carefully at Bella. "YOUR antennae have little knobs on the ends. That is WAY COOL! Mine are fuzzy, but if you REALLY want to see some fuzzy antenna, wait till you see Luna."

"Who's Luna?" Bella asked.

"Luna is the keeper of the woods," Morty answered. "She's a beautiful green moth who watches over us all night. Maybe she'll fly by before long."

Bella was starting to feel comfortable with her new friend. She relaxed and fluttered her wings for a moment. When she did, the bright orange on the tops of her wings flashed in the moonlight.

"Hey!" Morty cried. "I thought you were brown!"

"I've been keeping a little secret!" Bella giggled. "I'm orange on one side and brown on the other. I show the brown side to hide from PREDATORS that might want to eat me. But the orange side shows when I'm flying—and when I want to surprise a predator and scare it away."

"That is SO COOL!" Morty said. "Luna taught me about that. It's called FLASH COLORATION. It's when an animal uses bright color to surprise an enemy. I have a different kind of flash coloration. Can you guess where?" A little smile spread across Morty's face.

Bella looked closely at Morty and then asked him to turn around. He stepped carefully in a circle so she could see the top of his wings, but she didn't see any bright colors. "Okay, I give up," Bella said. "Where's the bright color?"

A ntennae are thin "feelers" on the heads some animals. Antennae are used for touching and smelling.

W hen animals use *flash coloration*, they suddenly display hidden bright colors to surprise an enemy.

Suddenly Morty flew off, and Bella saw patches of bright pink on his **HIND WINGS**. "Hey, how did you do that?" she called to him.

Morty flew back around and showed Bella how his hind wings tucked under his **FOREWINGS** when he was resting. "I hide my hind wings when I'm not flying. It's like having a secret weapon. Cool, hunh?"

"VERY cool!" Bella exclaimed.

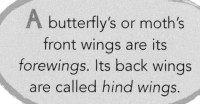

Morty added, "Luna also told me about **WARNING COLORATION**. That's when an animal has bright colors or patterns that show all the time and warn predators to keep away. The colorful animal might be poisonous or taste bad, for example. Keeping predators away helps the animal stay alive!"

Just then, a big green shape zipped by. It was Luna! She landed on the branch that the nest was on. Morty introduced Bella to her. "Luna, we have a diurnal visitor this evening. This is Bella the Butterfly. Bella, this is Luna. She's a luna moth."

"Welcome to our world, Bella," Luna said in a gentle voice.

A butterfly's or moth's front wings are its *forewings*. Its back wings are called *hind wings*.

An animal with *warning coloration* has easily seen bright colors to warn an enemy that it tastes bad or is poisonous.

Bella was speechless—she couldn't stop staring at Luna's antennae. She'd never seen anything like them in her whole life.

Luna blushed. "You must be looking at my antennae. I must admit, they're pretty fuzzy. Many, but not all, moths have fuzzy antennae. Butterflies have smooth antennae with knobs, like yours."

"Er, very nice to meet you, Luna!" Bella said. "How else are butterflies and moths different?"

Luna replied, "Well, you've probably already noticed that Morty is much fuzzier than you. His body is also thicker and heavier than yours. And did you notice that you rest with your wings in different positions? Morty's wings are spread out flat when he rests, but yours are raised above your body."

"What do you eat?" Bella asked. (She was hungry, but she didn't want to seem rude by asking for food.)

"Believe it or not," Luna began, "I don't eat at all. When I was a caterpillar, I ate a LOT, but I don't need any food as an adult. Some adult butterflies don't eat, either. But Morty drinks NECTAR—the sweet juice of flowers."

Morty added, "The woods have different light-colored flowers that I can see because they reflect the moonlight. Also, many of the flowers have a sweet scent, which I can 'smell' with my antennae and feet. When I land on a flower, I can suck up the nectar with my PROBOSCIS. I'm getting hungry just thinking about it!"

"Hey, I find my food that way, too, and I also have a proboscis!" said Bella. "But I only drink nectar if I can't find other food. I prefer tree sap, rotten fruit, and animal poop. Yum!"

> Moths rest with their wings flat. Butterflies rest with their wings held together above their bodies.

> A *proboscis* is a tube-shaped mouthpart on an insect that is used to drink *nectar* and other liquids.

proboscis extended
for feeding

proboscis curled up
when not in use

Bella added, "However, many of my butterfly friends drink nectar, which they find by sight, not smell. They're attracted to brightly colored flowers, which they can see during the day."

Morty said, "Do you want to see something really cool? Check out Luna's EYESPOTS! Luna, would you show them to Bella, please?"

Luna flew off the branch, and Bella saw two spots on her hind wings.

Luna explained, "My eyespots are for startling predators, and they've saved my life many times! They work a bit like flash coloration—by surprise. Some other moths have eyespots, too, and so do some butterflies. Many have much bigger eyespots!"

Bella loved talking with Luna and Morty, and she loved learning new things about the amazing world around her. But she was ready to go home—for now, anyway. She saw a thin line of orange on the horizon. The sun would be coming up soon, and she'd be able to find her way home.

Butterflies and moths may use sight, scent, or both to find food.

Many butterflies are attracted to colorful flower they can see in the day. Moths can see white flowers that reflect the moonlight.

Eyespots are eye-shaped markings that may surprise a predator and scare it away.

Luna and Morty both yawned. It was bedtime for both of them. Morty said, "We have to go get some sleep now. Can I see you again sometime?"

Bella said, "I have an idea! When you wake up, come to this tree right away. The sun will be going down then. I'll come here right before I go home, and we can play for a few minutes before I have to leave. We can see each other two times every day—at sunrise and sunset!"

"Great idea!" Morty replied with a grin. He was excited to see his new friend again so soon. "See you later!"

What are you CURIOUS about?

Day or Night?

After reading about Bella, Morty, and Luna, you know the time of day when each one is active. Bella is *diurnal*—she's active during the day. Morty and Luna are *nocturnal*—they're active at night. Most (but not all) butterflies are diurnal, and most (but not all) moths are nocturnal.

You now also know how to tell butterflies and moths apart. Moths have thick, fuzzy bodies and fuzzy antennae. Butterflies have thinner, smoother bodies and knobbed antennae. Remember that you *can't* tell them apart by eyespots or by blending, flash, or warning coloration because both butterflies and moths can have any of these.

Now it's time to put all your knowledge together and play a game!

INSTRUCTIONS

Object of the game:
Correctly match diurnal butterflies with each other and nocturnal moths with each other by recognizing physical traits that distinguish butterflies from moths.

1. Cut out the cards on page 31. Mix them up and place them face down in a loose pile in between the players on a table or other playing surface.

2. Player A draws the top three cards from the pile. Without letting other players see, Player A hides one piece of art face up under each of the three cups.

3. Player B lifts up two cups to try to make a match. He or she explains to the other players why the two cards match or don't match. For example, for the first picture in the top example on the next page, Player B might say, "This one has fuzzy antennae, so it's a moth. Most moths are active at night, so it's a match with the moon card."

> **MATERIALS**
>
> - Paper butterflies, moths, suns, and moons (cutouts on page 31)
> - Three opaque cups
> - Paper and pencil for scoring

Day or Night?

INSTRUCTIONS (continued)

Any of these pairs make a match:

butterfly – sun
moth – moon
butterfly – butterfly
moth – moth
sun – sun
moon – moon

Examples of a Match

NOTE: See pages 14 and 15 to meet some butterflies and moths! You can look at these if you get stuck!

4. Players get 1 point for a match.

5. Next, players get to see what is under the third cup. After turning over the third cup, players must figure out whether none, one, or both of the first two cards match the third card. If the player figures this out correctly (that is, correctly identifies how many of the first two cards match the third), he or she earns a new point. Players will earn a total of zero, one, or two points each turn.

6. Then the next player takes a turn.

7. The game ends when a player has 10 points. For a longer game, play to 25 points.

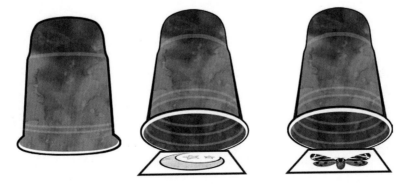

MEET SOME BUTTERFLIES!

Question mark

Gladiator

Eastern tiger swallowtail

Purple emperor

Zebra longwing

Malachite

Crimson rose

Monarch

Peacock

California sister

Little sulphur

Blue morpho

MEET SOME MOTHS!

White-lined sphinx

Luna

Reddish speckled dart

Rosy maple

Large tolype

Tuliptree silkmoth

Regal

Io

Lime hawkmoth

Similar underwing

Common white wave

Jersey tiger

Make a Butterfly or Moth

Think about the differences between butterflies and moths. Do you recognize fuzzy antennae when you see them? How about knobbed ones? Can you tell the difference between a thick, fuzzy body and a thinner, smoother one?

For this activity, you'll be choosing body parts of butterflies or moths that go together. For example, fuzzy antennae go with fuzzy bodies, right?

And what about the wings? MOST butterflies are brightly colored, and MOST moths have dull colors, but that's not always the case, and there are MANY exceptions. Fuzziness, antennae, and body thickness are better ways to tell the difference.

One last thing before you get started. Butterflies and moths are insects, so they each have six legs. However, their legs are so thin that it would be hard to cut them out and handle them for this activity, so we'll skip them. But keep in mind that a living butterfly or moth does have legs!

INSTRUCTIONS

1. Look at all the different butterflies and moths on the Meet Some Butterflies! and Meet Some Moths! pages (pages 14 and 15). Choose a favorite one for this craft activity or create one from your imagination!

2. Find the wing, body, and antennae shapes (pages 33, 35, 37) you'd like to use for this activity. Decorate those shapes with crayons, colored pencils, or markers to make them look however you want.

3. Cut out the parts you just colored. You might want to ask an adult to help you cut out the antennae.

4. Cut out the two rectangles at the bottom of page 37 and use them to trace two rectangles on lightweight cardboard (such as from the flap of a cereal box). Then cut out the cardboard rectangles,

MATERIALS

- Scissors
- Glue or tape (possibly double-sided tape)
- Small piece of lightweight cardboard (a cereal box flap works great)
- Nylon fishing line
- Crayons, colored pencils, or markers
- Beads, sequins, and yarn or colored string (optional)—will require glue
- Wooden embroidery hoop— the inside one without any metal (optional)

Make a Butterfly or Moth

INSTRUCTIONS (continued)

make an X with them, and glue or tape them together. NOTE: The cardboard X should fit inside the wings you chose so it doesn't show when you put the two sets of wings together. Trim the ends of the X if you need to so it is completely hidden. You will only need one piece of cardboard—*not* an X—for the smallest pair of moth wings.

5. Glue or tape the X to the back of the wings you cut out. By attaching the wings to the X, they will stay in place better than if you just attach the two sets of wings to each other.

6. Glue or tape the body on top of the line where the wings meet.

7. Glue or tape the antennae in place. You may want to attach them to the *underside* of the head (the side you didn't color in).

8. If you want your insect to look the same from every direction, color another set of *the same type of wings and body* to create an identical twin. Then glue or tape it on the back of the first one (on the other side of the cardboard X).

9. If you used glue, let it dry before proceeding to Step 10.

10. Gently crease your creation lengthwise from its head to the back tip of its body. The fold will help it look more real after you hang it.

11. Add any extra decorations you'd like, such as beads, sequins, and yarn or string.

12. To add a proboscis, cut out a long, thin rectangle of paper and roll most of it up tight. Then let it go so it loosens up. Glue or tape one end under the head of your butterfly or moth.

13. Ask an adult to help you use a needle to tie a piece of nylon fishing line to your creation. Then hang it in a place where you'll see it often!

Bonus Craft Ideas:
For a longer project, make several butterflies and moths and string them together—or create more of them and make a mobile by hanging them from a wooden embroidery hoop!

ACTIVITY
2

Make a Butterfly or Moth

FUN FACTS
ABOUT BUTTERFLIES AND MOTHS

Did you know that there's another way to tell butterflies and moths apart? Most moths have tiny hooks on their wings. The hooks hold each forewing to the hind wing so the wings can work together while the moth is flying. (VERY few butterflies have these hooks.) Check out this diagram:

MALE **FEMALE**

part of the forewing

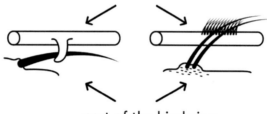

part of the hindwing

Keep in mind that these hooks are TINY—way too tiny to include in the drawings for this activity.

Butterflies have a different way to keep each forewing and hind wing working together. The front of each hind wing is lobe-shaped—large and round to overlap with the forewing.

Though moths and butterfly wings are usually built in these two different ways, it is safest to stick with body shape, antennae shape, and fuzziness to tell butterflies and moths apart.

lobe on the front of hind wing

(as seen from the underside of the butterfly)

ACTIVITY 3

Test Your Wings

In *Bella the Butterfly Meets Morty the Moth*, you read about several ways that animals use color and patterns to hide or escape from predators.

- Bella uses **BLENDING COLORATION** when she hides with her wings up and blends with the color of the nest.

- Morty uses **FLASH COLORATION** to surprise predators by showing the pink on his hind wings. (Bella also uses this when she suddenly flutters her wings.)

- Luna displays her **EYESPOTS** to startle predators and buy some extra time to escape.

- Morty also mentions **WARNING COLORATION**, which involves bright colors or patterns that are easily seen and warn predators to keep away.

Now it's time to pretend that you're a butterfly or moth that uses one of these four ways to stay safe! Will you hide, surprise, or warn?

INSTRUCTIONS

1. Assign one player to be the predator and everyone else to be a butterfly or moth.

2. Print out the eyespots on pages 39 and 41.

3. Using a hole punch, create a hole in the top of each pair of eyespots, where the circle is. If you don't have a hole punch, you can push a paper clip through the card. Tie a piece of string through the hole or paper clip to make the card into a necklace.

4. To start, each of the butterflies and moths will choose one of the four ways of staying safe.

MATERIALS

- One neutral-colored T-shirt for each player*

- One brightly colored T-shirt for each player*

- Hole punch (or a paper clip)

- Scissors

- String

*T-shirts should have the same length sleeves (both short or both long).

Test Your Wings

INSTRUCTIONS (continued)

Way of Staying Safe	What to Wear
Blending coloration	A neutral-colored or dark T-shirt (for example, beige, white, gray, brown, or black)
Flash coloration	A red or other brightly colored T-shirt that is hidden under a neutral or dark T-shirt
Eyespots	Eyespots (see cutouts) worn as a necklace
Warning coloration	A red or other brightly colored T-shirt that is visible

5. Now it's time for players to BECOME butterflies and moths. If you are a butterfly or moth, how will you move? Will you walk or run? Pretend you're swimming? Slither on the ground? NO! You'll ... yup, you got it—FLY!! So get those arms—oops, *wings*—warmed up!

"Fly" around outside or, if the weather isn't nice enough to play outdoors, fly more slowly in a large room. Pretend you're just minding your own business, looking for food.

Predators can be birds or mammals, flying through the air or walking on the ground, looking for food.

When butterflies and moths meet predators, it's time to display some protective behavior! **IF YOU'RE A BUTTERFLY OR MOTH,** display the behavior that matches the role you've taken on:

ACTIVITY 3

Test Your Wings

INSTRUCTIONS (continued)

Way of Staying Safe	Behavior
Blending coloration	Try to blend in
Flash coloration	Flash your bright color quickly by lifting your neutral t-shirt and showing the bright one.
Eyespots	Flash your eyespots by moving around quickly in front of the other person.
Warning coloration	Fly around confidently, as if you know you're scary!

IF YOU'RE A PREDATOR, respond in the proper way to the role your friend has taken on:

Way of Staying Safe	How to Respond
Blending coloration	Search for the insect, even if it's right in front of you.
Flash coloration	Look surprised and fly away.
Eyespots	Look surprised and fly away.
Warning coloration	Don't get too close; look concerned or scared.

6. Take a few moments to guess and talk about what each other is doing. If you're a predator, guess which role the butterfly or moth was playing. If you're a butterfly or moth, guess how the predator responded to you. Did you guess correctly what each other was doing?

7. After you've guessed and shared, switch! The predator will become a butterfly or moth, and one of the butterflies or moths will become the predator.

8. Continue playing until all players have had a turn to try out each role (type of coloration or behavior). Change T-shirts as appropriate when you take on a new role.

This isn't a game in the sense of winners and losers. Instead, it's an opportunity to have some fun while experiencing different ways that butterflies and moths stay safe.

EXTRA CHALLENGE: Each player yells out the type of coloration of the other player after seeing it. If they remembered it right the first time, they get a point. The first player to reach 10 points wins.

ACTIVITY
4

Butterflies and Moths in Your Area

INSTRUCTIONS

In this activity, you'll learn about butterflies and moths you may see where you live!

Part 1: Research

1. Search the Internet to find photos and information about butterflies and moths in your area. Check out this website:

   - http://enature.com – Click on "Butterflies" under Field Guides. Then choose a group of butterflies (for example, Swallowtails) to get to a page where you can select your region to narrow down the choices that are displayed. Under "Filters," you can select your region or even fill in your zip code. (Unfortunately, this site has no field guide for moths.)

   You may also find helpful resources by typing "common butterflies in _____" (your state or region) or "common moths in _____" in a search engine.

2. Read about different kinds of butterflies and moths that live in your area. Then choose two butterflies and two moths that you are curious about. You can make your choices by color, pattern, size, shape, behavior, or anything else that interests you!

3. Read to learn about each butterfly or moth, one at a time. Then, for each one, fill in a page of your Research Journal. (Make copies of the page so you have one sheet for each of the four insects you chose.) You may want to refer to the drawings below of the basic body plans of butterflies and moths.

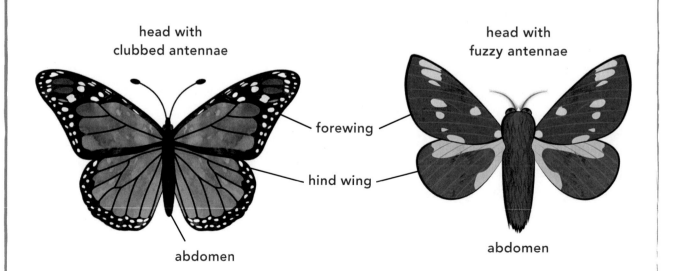

head with
clubbed antennae

forewing

hind wing

abdomen

head with
fuzzy antennae

abdomen

ACTIVITY 4

Butterflies and Moths in Your Area

INSTRUCTIONS (continued)

Part 2: Identification

This is a summertime activity. If it's not summer right now, mark your calendar!

Go outside at different times of the day and look for butterflies and moths. Take a notepad and a pencil or pen to record details you notice about each one you find. A small camera is also great to bring along.

NOTE: You may be able to see lots of moths after dark on a screen door or window screen or around an outdoor light. Moths often stay still on screens for a long enough time for you to study them and take pictures!

> ### MATERIALS
> - Notepad
> - Pencil or pen
> - Pocket or phone camera (optional)

1. When you see a butterfly or moth, stay still so you don't startle it. Notice its size and features. How big is it? (It's okay to estimate.) What color is it? Does it have unusual markings? Does it seem to prefer certain flowers or other food sources?

2. If possible, take a picture of the butterfly or moth.

3. Using your notes and any pictures you took, fill in as much information as you can on a page of your Field Journal for each butterfly or moth you see.

4. Try to identify the butterfly or moth using the online resources listed in Part 1 of this activity or by visiting this website:

   - http://bugguide.net/node/view/15740 – Click on the moth or butterfly under "Clickable Guide" in the top left area. Then scroll down to the "Identification" area to see photos and silhouettes of moths or butterflies.

   Another option is to register for a free account with the Butterflies and Moths of North America project and submit a photo, along with the date and location, to http://www. butterfliesandmoths.org/identify. If someone associated with the site can identify the type of butterfly or moth, you'll receive an email letting you know what kind you saw, and your photo will be added to the project's database of sightings. You can also submit photos and information for caterpillars!

ACTIVITY
4

Butterflies and Moths in Your Area

INSTRUCTIONS (continued)

5. Create a page of your Field Journal for each butterfly or moth you see—not just now, but also in the future. Include the dates of sightings. Imagine how many different types you will have seen a few years from now!

Don't Touch!

Butterflies and moths are really cool to look at, but it's best to avoid touching them. They depend on their wings to stay safe and get food, and any damage could lead to death. Similarly, if you catch a butterfly or moth in a small jar, it may damage its wings by flapping them against the glass.

If a butterfly or moth lands on you, stay still and watch it closely, but keep your hands to yourself!

Research Journal

Draw three pictures of the butterfly or moth:

- what it looks like when it's an adult

- what it looks like when it's a caterpillar

- what it looks like when it's a pupa

CATERPILLAR

ADULT

PUPA

What is the name of the butterfly or moth? _____

What is its wingspan (the distance from wingtip to wingtip)? _____

Where does it live? _____

When is it active? ☐ Diurnal   ☐ Nocturnal   ☐ Other _____

What does it eat? _____

Other interesting facts _____

_____

_____

ACTIVITY
4

Field Journal

Did you see a butterfly or moth? A caterpillar? A pupa?

Draw a picture of what you saw in the left-hand box.

If you took a photo, print it out and tape or glue it in the right-hand box.

Observations

Where did you see your bug? _____

Was it flying or sitting on something? _____

Was it eating? _____

What was the environment in which you found it (woods, fields, etc.)? _____

What time of year did you see it? _____

What time of day did you see it? _____

What website did you use to figure out what type it is? _____

What type do you think it is? _____

Curiosity Connector

Here are some links to help you follow your curiosity!

- Do you have lots of questions about butterflies and moths? Find answers here:
  http://www.kidsbutterfly.org/faq

- Watch a cool video clip about butterflies and moths here:
  http://video.nationalgeographic.com/video/kids/animals-pets-kids/bugs-kids/butterflies-kids/

  And many more here:
  http://www.bbc.co.uk/nature/life/Lepidoptera

- Are you looking for more fun butterfly activities? Find them here:
  http://butterflywebsite.com/

- Learn about attracting butterflies to a garden here:
  http://www.nwf.org/How-to-Help/Garden-for-Wildlife/Gardening-Tips/How-to-Attract-Butterflies-to-Your-Garden.aspx

- Learn about the life cycle of butterflies and moths here:
  http://www.ansp.org/explore/online-exhibits/butterflies/lifecycle/

- The eggs and caterpillars of butterflies and moths are almost as pretty (and different) as the adults! See some amazing photos here:
  http://www.ukleps.org/morphology.html

What are you CURIOUS about?

Glossary

ANTENNAE — thin, sensitive feelers on the heads of insects and some other animals that are used for touch and smell

BLENDING COLORATION — a type of camouflage that helps some animals blend in with their surroundings and hide from predators

CAMOUFLAGE — colors, patterns, or shapes that protect some animals from being attacked by making them hard to see in their surroundings

DIURNAL — active during the daytime

EYESPOTS — large spots on an animal that look like eyes and that may distract predators that are pursuing the animal

FLASH COLORATION — an area of bright color on a dull-colored animal that is only seen when the animal is moving and that may distract predators that are pursuing the animal

FOREWINGS — the front wings of an insect that has four wings

HIND WINGS — the back wings of an insect that has four wings

NECTAR — a sweet liquid made by flowering plants

NOCTURNAL — active at night

PREDATORS — animals that hunt and eat other animals for food

PROBOSCIS — a long, thin tube that some insects, including butterflies and moths, use for drinking

WARNING COLORATION — easily noticed coloring that tells other animals that an animal is poisonous or tastes bad

Tools for Your Tool Kit

Let's make the ideas you learned today part of your life tool kit. Remember to print out some blank tool kit pages and tape or glue on today's tools.

1. When are most butterflies active? _____

   Add DIURNAL to your tool kit!

2. When are most moths active? _____

   Add NOCTURNAL to your tool kit!

3. How do Bella and Morty drink nectar from flowers? _____

   Add PROBOSCIS to your tool kit!

4. Why did Bella choose to hide in the empty bird's nest? _____

   _____

   Add BLENDING COLORATION to your tool kit!

5. What is the purpose of the patches of bright pink on Morty's hind wings?

   _____

   _____

   Add FLASH COLORATION to your tool kit!

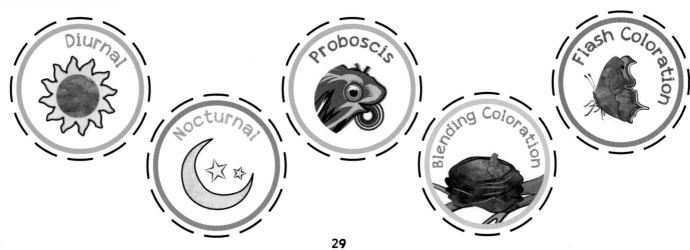

Cutouts for Activity 1: Day or Night?

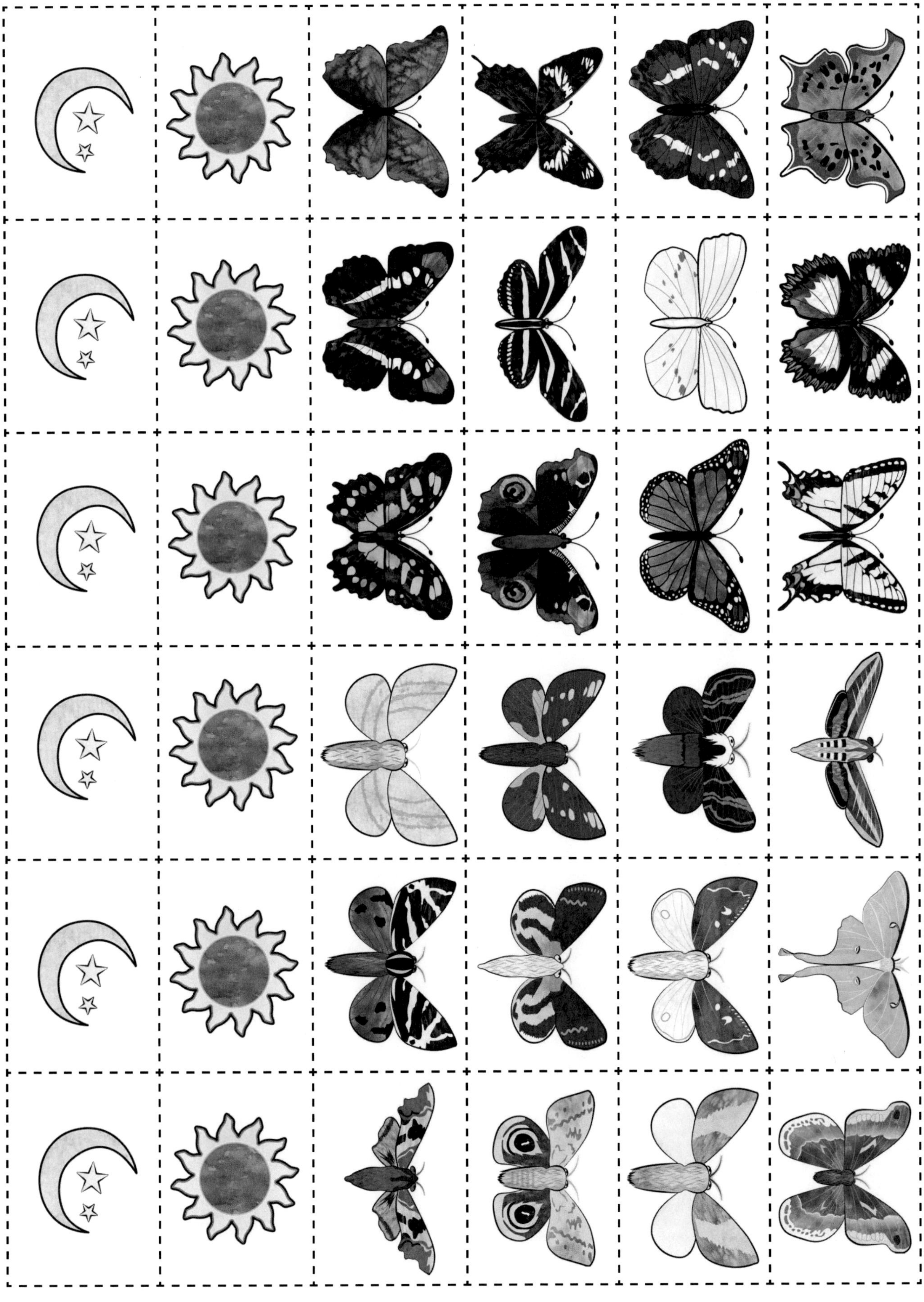

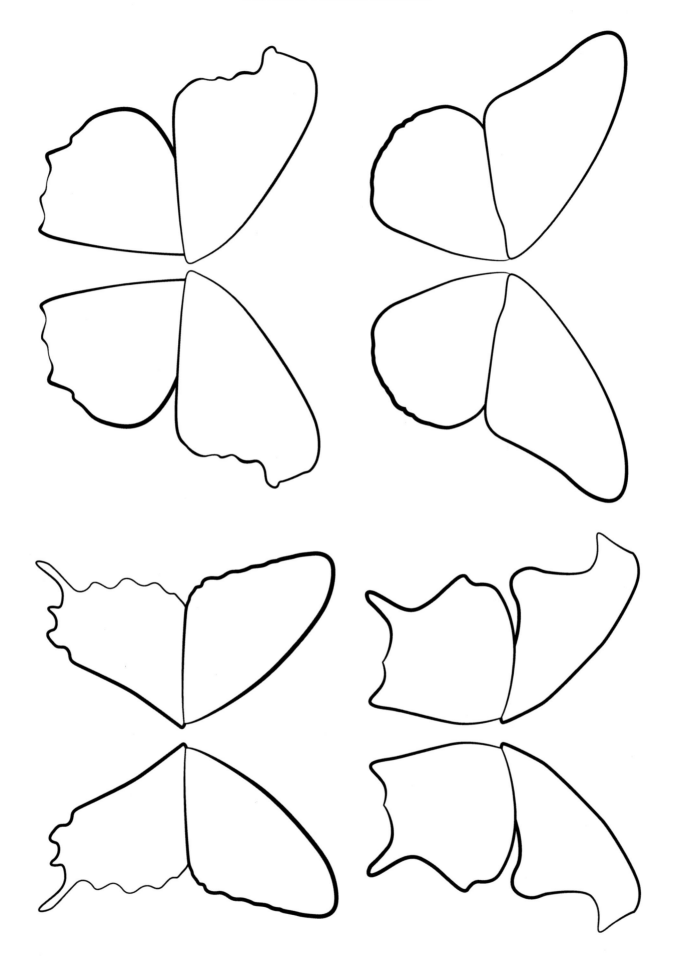

Cutouts for Activity 2: Make a Butterfly or Moth

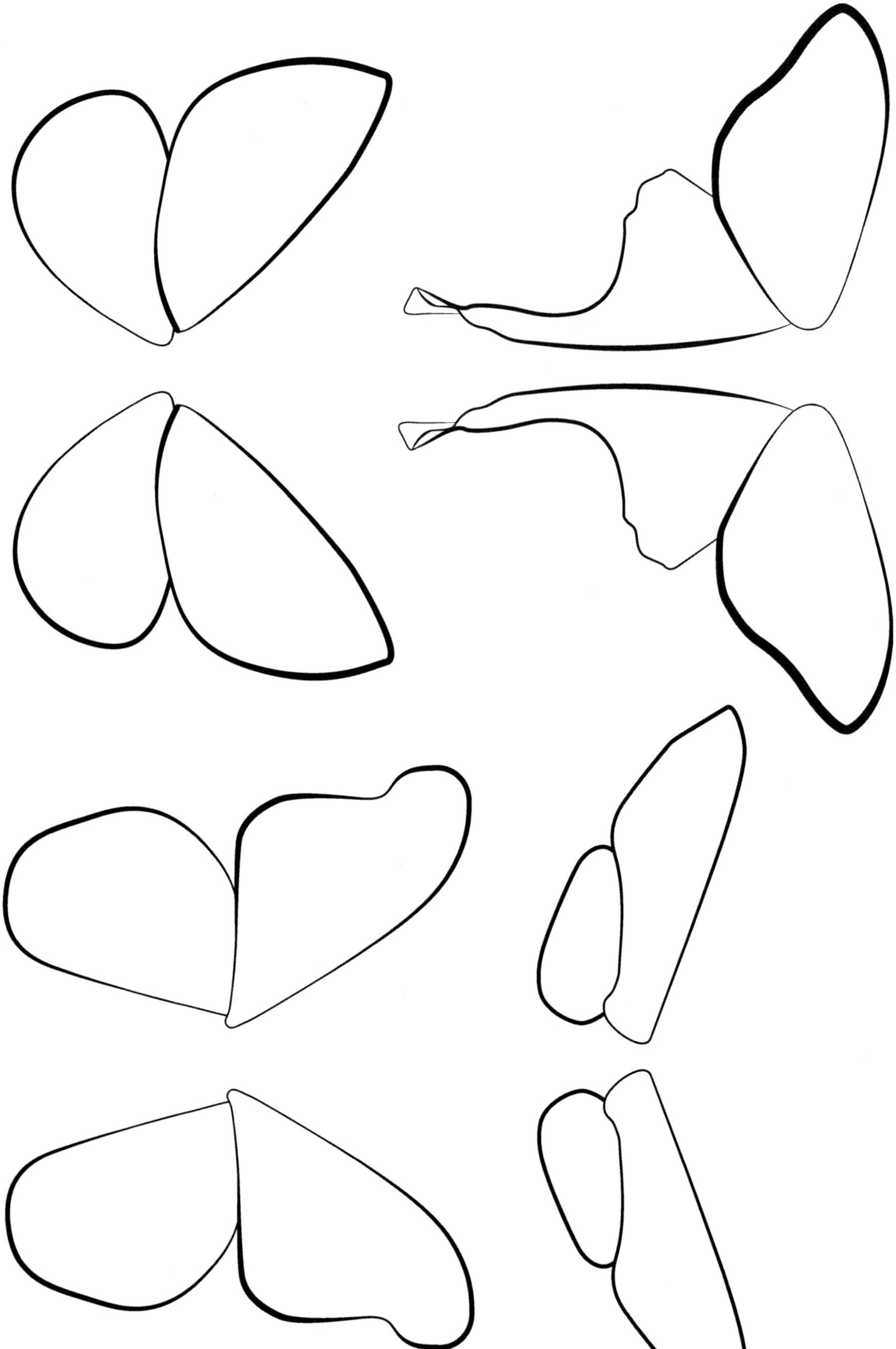

Cutouts for Activity 2: Make a Butterfly or Moth

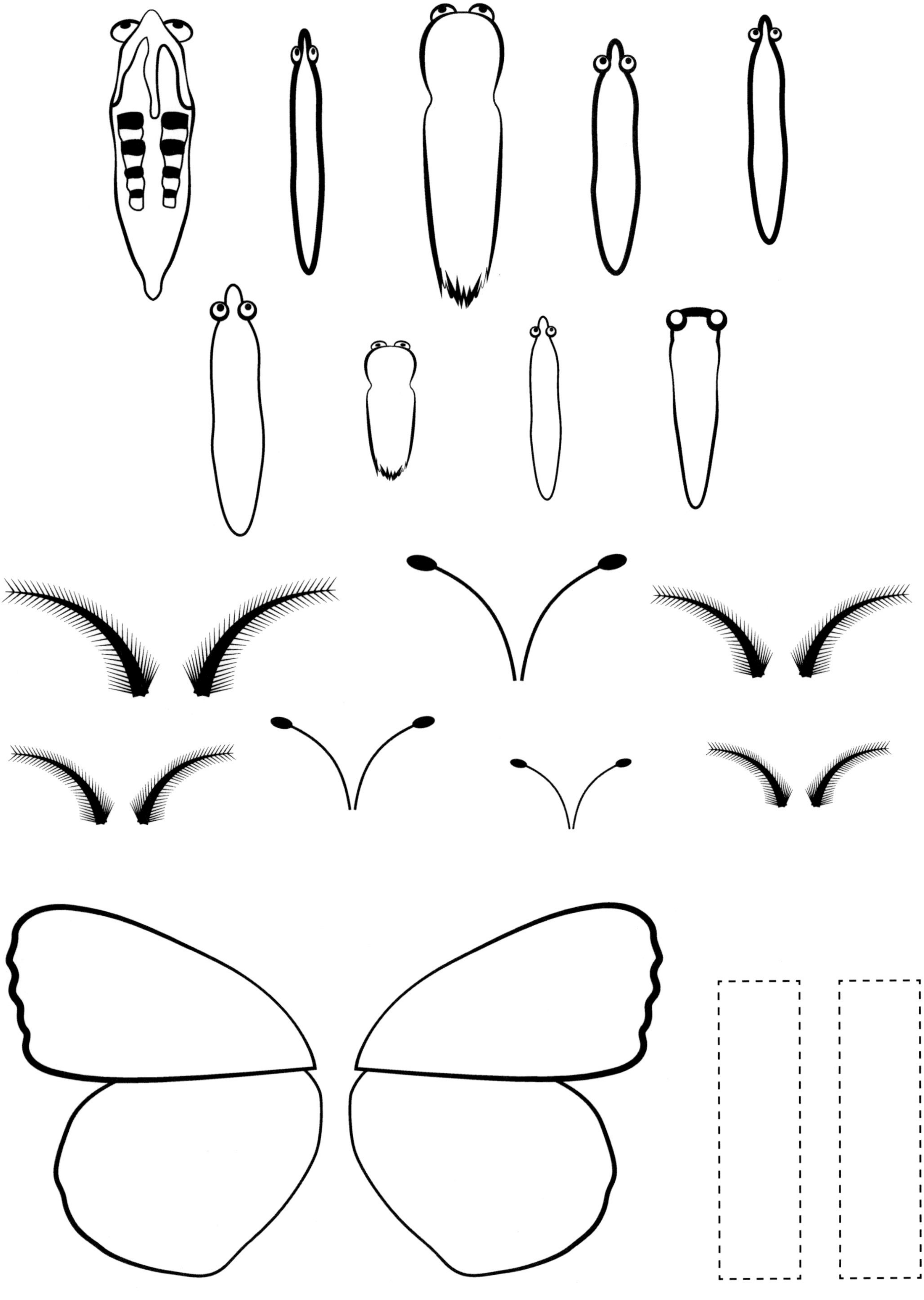

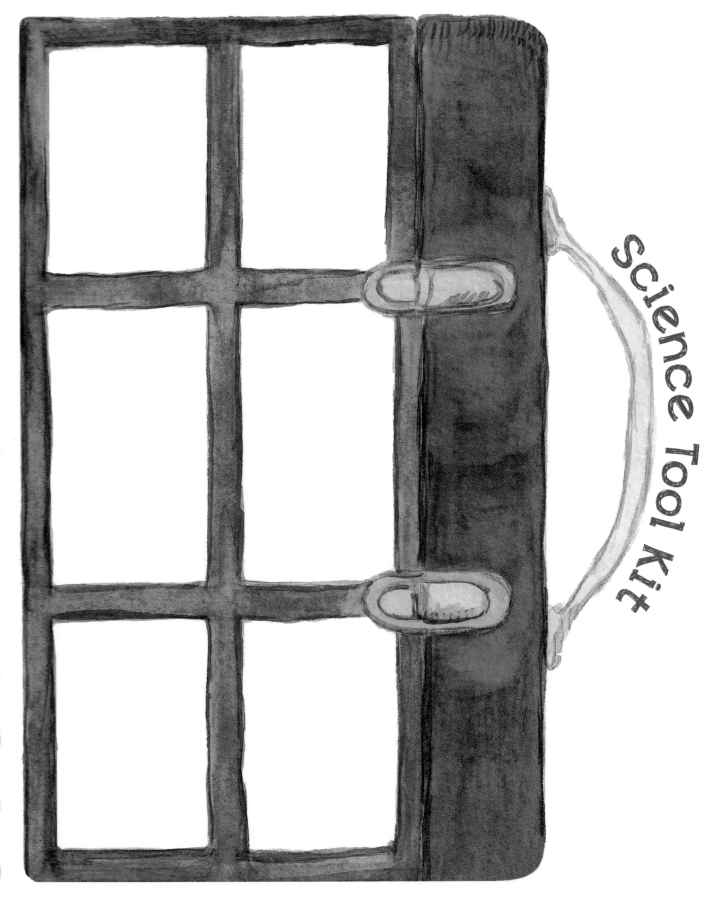

Science Tool Kit

Made in the USA
Lexington, KY
09 March 2018